contents

NZ, Canada, US and UK readers
Please note: Australian cup and spoon measurements are metric. A conversion chart appears on page 63.

lemon chicken

4 single chicken breast fillets (680g)
2 egg whites, beaten lightly
½ cup (75g) plain flour
30g butter
2 tablespoons vegetable oil
1½ tablespoons cornflour
1 tablespoon brown sugar
½ cup (125ml) lemon juice
½ teaspoon grated fresh ginger
1 teaspoon soy sauce
1 cup (250ml) chicken stock

Using a meat mallet, gently pound chicken between sheets of plastic wrap until 1cm thick.
Dip chicken in egg white. Coat in flour; shake off excess flour.
Heat butter and oil in large frying pan; cook chicken, in batches, until browned both sides and cooked through. Drain on absorbent paper.
Meanwhile, blend cornflour and sugar with juice in small saucepan. Add ginger, sauce and stock; bring to a boil. Boil, stirring, until sauce thickens.
Slice chicken; serve drizzled with sauce.

serves 4
per serving 25.3g fat; 2011kJ (481 cal)
on the table in 30 minutes

garlic chicken stir-fry with bok choy

700g chicken breast fillets, sliced thinly
½ cup (75g) plain flour
2 tablespoons peanut oil
6 cloves garlic, crushed
1 medium red capsicum (200g), sliced thinly
6 green onions, sliced thinly
½ cup (125ml) chicken stock
2 tablespoons light soy sauce
500g bok choy, chopped coarsely

Coat chicken in flour; shake off excess.
Heat oil in wok or large frying pan; stir-fry chicken, in batches, until browned all over and cooked through.
Add garlic, capsicum and onion to wok; stir-fry until capsicum is tender.
Return chicken to wok with stock and sauce; stir-fry until sauce boils and thickens slightly. Just before serving, add bok choy; stir-fry until bok choy just wilts.

serves 4
per serving 20.4g fat; 1838kJ (440 cal)
on the table in 25 minutes
tip You can substitute any Asian green for the bok choy.

yakitori chicken

Mirin is a somewhat sweet rice wine used in many Asian, especially Japanese, dishes. You can substitute sherry or sweet white wine for mirin, if you prefer.

1kg chicken breast fillets
¼ cup (60ml) mirin
½ cup (125ml) light soy sauce
2cm piece fresh ginger (10g), grated finely
2 cloves garlic, crushed
¼ teaspoon ground black pepper
1 tablespoon sugar

Cut chicken into 2cm pieces.
Combine chicken with remaining ingredients in large bowl; stand 10 minutes. Drain chicken over small bowl; reserve marinade.
Thread chicken onto 12 bamboo skewers. Cook skewers on heated oiled grill plate (or grill or barbecue), turning and brushing with reserved marinade occasionally. Cook until yakitori are browned all over and cooked through.

serves 4
per serving 13.8g fat; 1614kJ (386 cal)
on the table in 35 minutes

chicken and tamarind stir-fry

Tamarind concentrate, a thick, purple-black, ready-to-use sweet-sour
paste manufactured from the pulp of tamarind tree pods, is available
from most supermarkets and Asian food stores.

700g chicken breast fillets, sliced thinly
1 tablespoon tamarind concentrate
3 cloves garlic, crushed
2 small fresh red thai chillies, sliced thinly
2 teaspoons sugar
1 tablespoon lime juice
1 tablespoon peanut oil
1 large brown onion (200g), sliced thickly
½ cup loosely packed fresh coriander leaves

Combine chicken, tamarind, garlic, chilli, sugar
and juice in medium bowl.
Heat half of the oil in wok or large frying pan; stir-fry
chicken mixture, in batches, until browned all over
and cooked through.
Heat remaining oil in wok; stir-fry onion until
just softened. Return chicken to wok; toss
gently to combine.
Serve chicken mixture sprinkled with coriander,
and steamed jasmine rice, if desired.

serves 4
per serving 8.7g fat; 1085kJ (259 cal)
on the table in 25 minutes

peanut-crusted thai chicken with cucumber salad

1 cup (150g) roasted
  unsalted peanuts
¼ cup (75g) red curry paste
1 tablespoon kecap manis
½ cup (125ml) coconut milk
1 cup coarsely chopped
  fresh coriander
4 single chicken
  breast fillets (680g)
1 telegraph cucumber (400g)
2 cups (160g) bean sprouts
⅓ cup coarsely chopped
  fresh mint
1 medium red onion (170g),
  halved, sliced thinly
1 teaspoon fish sauce
2 tablespoons
  sweet chilli sauce
1 tablespoon lime juice
1 tablespoon peanut oil

Preheat oven to moderately hot.
Blend or process peanuts, paste, kecap manis, coconut milk and half of the coriander until just combined.
Place chicken, in single layer, on oiled oven tray; spread peanut mixture on each piece. Roast, uncovered, in moderately hot oven about 20 minutes or until chicken is cooked through. Remove chicken from oven; cover, stand 5 minutes, slice thickly.
Meanwhile, cut cucumber in half lengthways. Remove and discard seeds; slice thinly. Combine cucumber in large bowl with sprouts, mint, onion and remaining coriander.
Combine the sauces, juice and oil in screw-top jar; shake well. Pour dressing over cucumber salad; toss gently to combine. Serve chicken topped with salad.

serves 4
per serving 44.6g fat; 2749kJ (658 cal)
on the table in 30 minutes

almond chicken and noodles

700g chicken breast fillets, sliced thickly
2 cloves garlic, crushed
¼ cup (60ml) hoisin sauce
¼ cup (60ml) kecap manis
2 tablespoons peanut oil
½ cup (80g) blanched almonds
4 green onions, sliced thinly
1 medium brown onion (150g), sliced thinly
420g fresh egg noodles
200g choy sum, chopped coarsely
1 cup (250ml) chicken stock

Combine chicken, garlic, 2 tablespoons of the hoisin sauce and 1 tablespoon of the kecap manis in medium bowl.
Heat 2 teaspoons of the oil in wok or large frying pan; stir-fry almonds until browned. Remove from wok.
Heat remaining oil in wok; stir-fry chicken mixture and onions, in batches, until chicken is browned.
Place noodles in large heatproof bowl, cover with boiling water, stand 5 minutes or until just tender; drain.
Return chicken to wok with almonds, noodles, choy sum, stock and remaining hoisin sauce and kecap manis; stir-fry until choy sum is just wilted.

serves 4
per serving 26.7g fat; 3049kJ (728 cal)
on the table in 20 minutes

american chicken salad

1½ cups (375ml) chicken stock
½ cup (125ml) water
700g chicken breast fillets
1 small baguette (165g), sliced thinly
2 tablespoons vegetable oil
¾ cup (225g) mayonnaise
½ cup (120g) sour cream
2 tablespoons lemon juice
3 trimmed celery stalks (300g), sliced thinly
1 medium white onion (150g), chopped finely
⅔ cup (110g) thinly sliced dill pickles
2 tablespoons finely chopped fresh flat-leaf parsley
1 tablespoon finely chopped fresh tarragon
1 large butter lettuce, leaves separated

Combine stock and the water in medium shallow
saucepan; bring to a boil.
Add chicken and simmer, loosely covered, about
8 minutes, turning once, until chicken is cooked through.
Remove chicken from pan; stand 10 minutes before slicing.
Meanwhile, brush bread slices with oil, toast until golden.
Combine mayonnaise, cream and juice in small bowl,
whisk until combined.
Combine chicken, mayonnaise mixture, celery, onion,
pickles and herbs in large bowl; mix well.
Serve in lettuce leaves with toasted bread slices.

serves 4
per serving 38.8g fat; 2959kJ (707 cal)
on the table in 35 minutes

honey chilli chicken salad

You will need two bunches of asparagus and a quarter of a medium chinese cabbage for this recipe.

500g chicken breast fillets, sliced thinly
¼ cup (90g) honey
4 small fresh red thai chillies, seeded, sliced thinly
4cm piece fresh ginger (20g), grated finely
400g asparagus, trimmed
2 tablespoons peanut oil
4 green onions, sliced thinly
1 medium green capsicum (200g), sliced thinly
1 medium yellow capsicum (200g), sliced thinly
1 medium carrot (120g), sliced thinly
150g chinese cabbage, shredded finely
⅓ cup (80ml) lime juice

Combine chicken, honey, chilli and ginger in medium bowl.
Cut asparagus spears in half; boil, steam or microwave until just tender. Rinse immediately under cold water; drain.
Meanwhile, heat half of the oil in wok or large frying pan; stir-fry chicken mixture, in batches, until browned all over and cooked through.
Place chicken and asparagus in large bowl with onion, capsicums, carrot, cabbage, juice and remaining oil; toss gently to combine.

serves 4
per serving 20.9g fat; 1704kJ (408 cal)
on the table in 25 minutes

chicken stir-fry on noodle cakes

3 x 85g packets chicken-flavoured instant noodles
2 tablespoons peanut oil
700g chicken breast fillets, sliced thinly
1 small brown onion (100g), sliced thinly
1 clove garlic, crushed
1 medium carrot (120g), sliced thinly
1 large red capsicum (350g), sliced thinly
400g baby bok choy, quartered
2cm piece fresh ginger (10g), grated finely
⅓ cup (80ml) oyster sauce
2 tablespoons soy sauce
¾ cup (180ml) chicken stock
1 tablespoon cornflour

Cook noodles following the instructions on packet. Drain noodles, add one of the flavour sachets and stir to combine (reserve remaining sachets for another use). Heat half of the oil in large frying pan, add noodles and press into a "cake" shape. Cook until browned on both sides.

Meanwhile, heat remaining oil in wok or large frying pan; stir-fry chicken, in batches, until cooked through.

Add onion and garlic to wok; stir-fry until just tender. Add carrot and capsicum; stir-fry until just tender.

Return chicken to wok with bok choy and combined ginger, sauces, stock and cornflour; stir-fry until mixture boils and thickens.

Cut noodle cake into quarters. Serve stir-fry on noodle cakes.

serves 4
per serving 25.8g fat; 2633kJ (629 cal)
on the table in 20 minutes

chicken, asparagus and potatoes in garlic cream sauce

Kipfler potatoes, small and finger-shaped, have a nutty flavour and are great baked or in salads. You will need two bunches of asparagus for this recipe.

500g kipfler potatoes,
halved lengthways
1 teaspoon cracked
black pepper
1 tablespoon olive oil
4 single chicken
breast fillets (680g)
400g asparagus,
trimmed
6 slices prosciutto (90g),
chopped coarsely
1 clove garlic, crushed
½ cup (125ml)
dry white wine
2 tablespoons
wholegrain mustard
300ml cream
¼ cup coarsely chopped
fresh chives

Preheat oven to hot.

Combine potato, pepper and oil in large bowl; mix well. Place potato, in single layer, on oiled oven tray; roast, uncovered, in hot oven about 20 minutes or until browned.

Meanwhile, heat large lightly oiled frying pan; cook chicken, in batches, until browned both sides. Place chicken, in single layer, on oven tray; roast, uncovered, in hot oven with potatoes about 10 minutes or until cooked through.

Remove chicken and potato from oven; cover, stand 5 minutes; slice chicken thickly.

Meanwhile, boil, steam or microwave asparagus until just tender; drain. Cover to keep warm.

Cook prosciutto in same frying pan, stirring, until just crisp. Remove from pan; cover to keep warm. Add garlic to pan; cook, stirring over low heat, until fragrant. Add wine; bring to a boil. Boil, stirring, until reduced to about 2 tablespoons. Add mustard and cream; bring to a boil. Boil, stirring, until mixture thickens slightly. Stir in chives.

Divide asparagus among serving plates; top with potato, half of the prosciutto, chicken, sauce, then remaining prosciutto.

serves 4
per serving 48.4g fat; 3039kJ (727 cal)
on the table in 30 minutes

thai-style steamed chicken with noodles

4 large silverbeet leaves
4 single chicken breast
  fillets (680g)
2 kaffir lime leaves,
  shredded finely
2 small fresh red thai chillies,
  seeded, sliced thinly
1 tablespoon finely
  chopped lemon grass
500g fresh rice noodles
sweet chilli dressing
¼ cup (60ml) sweet
  chilli sauce
2 teaspoons fish sauce
1 tablespoon lime juice
1 clove garlic, crushed
2 tablespoons finely
  chopped fresh coriander

Drop silverbeet into a pan of boiling water, drain immediately, then dip into a bowl of iced water until cold; drain well.

Place a chicken fillet on a silverbeet leaf, sprinkle with lime leaves, chilli and lemon grass. Wrap silverbeet around chicken to enclose.

Line a bamboo steamer with baking paper or a heatproof plate. Place chicken in prepared steamer over a wok or pan of simmering water. Cover and steam about 15 minutes or until cooked through.

Meanwhile, place noodles in large heatproof bowl, cover with hot water and stand for 5 minutes; drain.

Toss half of the sweet chilli dressing through noodles. Serve sliced chicken with noodles and remaining sweet chilli dressing.

sweet chilli dressing Combine ingredients in small bowl.

serves 4
per serving 4.9g fat; 1421kJ (339 cal)
on the table in 35 minutes

lemon and anchovy chicken with garlic pumpkin

800g piece butternut pumpkin, peeled
2 tablespoons olive oil
4 cloves garlic, sliced thinly
½ cup (125ml) chicken stock
12 fresh sage leaves
4 single chicken breast fillets (680g)
40g butter
3 anchovy fillets, drained, chopped finely
1 tablespoon lemon juice

Chop pumpkin into 1.5cm pieces. Heat half of the oil in large saucepan, add pumpkin and garlic; cook, stirring, until pumpkin begins to brown. Add 2 tablespoons of the stock; cover and steam for 5 minutes or until pumpkin is just tender. Stir in sage.

Meanwhile, cut chicken in half horizontally to give 8 thin pieces. Melt half of the butter and remaining oil in large frying pan; add chicken and cook until browned on both sides and just cooked through. Remove chicken from pan; keep warm.

Add remaining butter to same pan with anchovy; cook, stirring, until butter melts.

Add lemon juice and remaining stock; simmer, uncovered, 1 minute or until reduced slightly.

Serve pumpkin topped with chicken and sauce. Serve with rocket or a green salad, if desired.

serves 4
per serving 22.9g fat; 1844kJ (440 cal)
on the table in 25 minutes

rosemary, brie and sun-dried tomato chicken with corn mash

30g sun-dried tomatoes, chopped finely
1 tablespoon finely chopped fresh rosemary
4 single chicken breast fillets (680g)
60g firm brie, quartered
1kg medium new potatoes, quartered
2 cloves garlic, crushed
2 tablespoons milk
2 tablespoons sour cream
310g can creamed corn

Combine tomato and rosemary in small bowl.
Using a small sharp knife, slit a pocket in one side
of each chicken fillet, taking care not to cut all the
way through. Divide tomato mixture and brie among
pockets; secure openings with toothpicks.
Cook chicken on heated oiled grill plate (or grill or
barbecue) until browned both sides and cooked
through; cover to keep warm.
Meanwhile, boil, steam or microwave potato
until tender; drain. Mash potato in large bowl with
garlic, milk and sour cream; fold in corn. Serve
chicken with mash.

serves 4
per serving 13.8g fat; 2218kJ (530 cal)
on the table in 45 minutes

grilled chicken with herbed butter, almonds and gruyère

80g butter, softened
1 tablespoon finely chopped fresh flat-leaf parsley
2 teaspoons lemon juice
4 single chicken breast fillets (680g)
3 medium carrots (360g), cut into 8cm-long matchsticks
250g baby green beans
¼ cup (35g) toasted slivered almonds
¼ cup (30g) finely grated gruyère cheese

Combine butter, parsley and juice in small bowl, cover; refrigerate.

Cook chicken on heated oiled grill plate (or grill or barbecue) until browned both sides and cooked through. Cover loosely to keep warm.

Meanwhile, boil, steam or microwave carrot and beans, separately, until tender; drain.

Serve chicken on vegetables; divide parsley butter among chicken pieces, sprinkle with nuts and cheese.

serves 4
per serving 33.1g fat; 2061kJ (492 cal)
on the table in 35 minutes

even easier breasts

chicken tikka with cucumber-mint raita

Brush breast fillets with prepared tikka paste. Grill or barbecue until browned all over and cooked through. Serve with combined yogurt, peeled, seeded and finely chopped lebanese cucumber, chopped fresh mint and a pinch of ground cumin.

spiced chicken

Dip breast fillets into combined plain flour, ground cumin, coriander and salt. Heat olive oil in large frying pan; cook chicken until crisp and cooked through. Serve with a mixture of salad leaves, if desired.

chicken with mustard and rosemary

Combine breast fillets with wholegrain mustard, lemon juice, olive oil, finely chopped fresh rosemary and crushed garlic, stand 10 minutes; grill or barbecue until browned all over and cooked through.

chicken with coriander and chilli sauce

Blend or process chopped green onions, garlic, seeded and chopped red thai chillies, chopped coriander roots, brown sugar, lemon juice and a little fish sauce until well combined. Serve mixture spooned over grilled or barbecued breast fillets.

chicken breasts with citrus glaze

Cook breast fillets in heated oiled non-stick frying pan until browned and cooked through; remove from pan. Add strips of orange rind, orange juice, chicken stock and sweet orange marmalade to pan, bring to a boil; simmer, stirring, until thickened slightly. Return chicken to pan, turn to coat in glaze.

cajun chicken with mango salsa

Sprinkle breast fillets with prepared cajun seasoning; cook on heated oiled barbecue until browned and cooked through. Serve topped with combined finely chopped mango, tomato, red onion, crushed garlic, chopped fresh basil and a little balsamic vinegar.

chicken caesar salad

Arrange torn cos lettuce, poached and chopped breast fillets, chopped and fried bacon and toasted bread cubes in large bowl. Top with flaked parmesan cheese and drained anchovy fillets, then drizzle with prepared caesar salad dressing.

sweet paprika chicken with chickpea salad

Combine breast fillets, ground turmeric, sweet paprika, finely grated lemon rind, crushed garlic and olive oil; stand 10 minutes. Cook chicken in heated oiled non-stick frying pan until browned and cooked through. Meanwhile, combine chopped fresh tomato, rinsed and drained canned chickpeas, chopped fresh flat-leaf parsley, lemon juice and olive oil. Serve chicken with chickpea salad.

portuguese-style chicken thighs

2 teaspoons cracked black pepper
1 teaspoon dried oregano leaves
2 small fresh red thai chillies, seeded, chopped finely
½ teaspoon hot paprika
1 clove garlic, crushed
¼ cup (60ml) red wine vinegar
¼ cup (60ml) olive oil
6 chicken thigh fillets (660g), halved

Combine pepper, oregano, chilli, paprika, garlic, vinegar and oil in medium bowl. Reserve about a quarter of the spicy mixture in small jug; use hands to rub remaining spicy mixture onto chicken pieces.
Cook chicken, in batches, on heated oiled grill plate (or grill or barbecue) until browned both sides and cooked through.
Serve chicken drizzled with reserved spicy mixture.

serves 4
per serving 25.6g fat; 1496kJ (357 cal)
on the table in 25 minutes

chicken chermoulla

Chermoulla is a Moroccan blend of herbs and spices traditionally used for preserving or seasoning meat and fish. We used our chermoulla blend here as a quick baste for chicken, but you can also make it for use as a sauce or marinade.

700g chicken thigh fillets, sliced thinly
½ cup coarsely chopped fresh flat-leaf parsley
1 tablespoon finely grated lemon rind
1 tablespoon lemon juice
2 teaspoons ground turmeric
½ teaspoon cayenne pepper
1 tablespoon ground coriander
1 medium red onion (170g), chopped finely
2 tablespoons olive oil
1 cup (200g) red lentils
2½ cups (625ml) chicken stock
200g baby spinach leaves
½ cup coarsely chopped fresh coriander
½ cup coarsely chopped fresh mint
1 tablespoon red wine vinegar
⅓ cup (95g) yogurt

Combine chicken, parsley, rind, juice, spices, onion and half of the oil in large bowl. Heat wok or large frying pan; stir-fry chicken mixture, in batches, until chicken is browned and cooked through.
Meanwhile, combine lentils and stock in medium saucepan. Bring to a boil; reduce heat. Simmer, uncovered, about 8 minutes or until just tender; drain. Place lentils in large bowl with spinach, coriander, mint and combined vinegar and remaining oil; toss gently to combine.
Serve chicken mixture on lentil mixture; drizzle with yogurt.

serves 4
per serving 24.9g fat; 2191kJ (524 cal)
on the table in 30 minutes

warm chicken and coriander salad

1 tablespoon peanut oil
¼ cup (35g) slivered almonds
700g chicken thigh fillets, sliced thickly
2 tablespoons finely chopped fresh coriander
1 small red capsicum (150g), chopped coarsely
2 trimmed celery stalks (200g), chopped coarsely
250g cherry tomatoes, halved
1 medium avocado (250g), chopped coarsely
3 green onions, chopped coarsely
1 baby cos lettuce, chopped coarsely
dressing
⅓ cup (100g) mayonnaise
⅓ cup (85g) sour cream
2 tablespoons lemon juice

Heat oil in large frying pan, add nuts; cook, stirring, until nuts are browned lightly, remove from pan. Reheat oil; cook chicken, stirring, until cooked through. Drain on absorbent paper.
Combine nuts, chicken, coriander, capsicum, celery and dressing; gently stir in tomato, avocado, onion and lettuce.
dressing Combine ingredients in small bowl; mix well.

serves 4
per serving 48.7g fat; 2651kJ (633 cal)
on the table in 30 minutes

spicy chicken with rice noodles

700g chicken thigh fillets, chopped coarsely
2 cloves garlic, crushed
2cm piece fresh ginger (10g), grated finely
2 teaspoons finely chopped fresh lemon grass
1 tablespoon teriyaki sauce
1 tablespoon sugar
1 teaspoon sambal oelek
1 teaspoon ground cumin
1 teaspoon ground coriander
500g fresh wide rice noodles
2 tablespoons sweet chilli sauce
1 tablespoon peanut oil
500g baby bok choy, quartered

Combine chicken, garlic, ginger, lemon grass, teriyaki sauce, sugar, sambal and spices in medium bowl.
Rinse noodles in strainer under hot water. Separate with fork; drain. Place noodles in medium bowl; combine with sweet chilli sauce.
Meanwhile, heat half of the oil in wok or large frying pan; stir-fry chicken mixture, in batches, until chicken is browned all over and cooked through.
Heat remaining oil in wok; stir-fry bok choy until just wilted.
Serve chicken mixture with bok choy and noodles.

serves 4
per serving 18.2g fat; 1895kJ (453 cal)
on the table in 25 minutes
tip If you can't find fresh rice noodles, the chicken and bok choy can be served on a bed of steamed rice.

chicken and snake beans with holy basil

In this dish we've used holy basil, also known as kra pao or hot basil. If you can't find it, use ordinary sweet basil instead. Snake beans are long, thin green beans that are Asian in origin; if unavailable, you can use green beans.

700g snake beans
1 tablespoon peanut oil
700g chicken thigh fillets, chopped coarsely
2 medium white onions (300g), sliced thickly
3 cloves garlic, crushed
1 teaspoon five-spice powder
½ cup (125ml) oyster sauce
2 tablespoons light soy sauce
½ cup (75g) cashew nuts, toasted
½ cup loosely packed holy basil leaves

Cut snake beans into 5cm lengths.
Heat half of the oil in wok or large frying pan; stir-fry chicken, in batches, until browned all over and cooked through.
Heat remaining oil in wok; stir-fry onion, garlic and five-spice until onion softens. Add beans; stir-fry until beans are tender.
Return chicken to wok with sauces and nuts; stir-fry until sauce boils and thickens slightly. Just before serving, stir in basil.

serves 4
per serving 27.7g fat; 2087kJ (498 cal)
on the table in 20 minutes

chicken and bean madras

1 tablespoon peanut oil
1 large white onion (200g), sliced thinly
700g chicken thigh fillets, sliced thinly
¼ cup (75g) madras curry paste
200g green beans, chopped coarsely
½ cup (125ml) chicken stock
1 tablespoon tomato paste

Heat oil in wok or large frying pan; stir-fry onion and chicken, in batches, until chicken is just browned.
Heat curry paste in wok; stir-fry until fragrant. Return chicken mixture to wok with beans, stock and tomato paste; stir-fry until sauce thickens slightly and chicken is cooked through.
Serve with steamed basmati rice, if desired.

serves 4
per serving 23.3g fat; 1570kJ (375 cal)
on the table in 25 minutes

even easier thighs

chicken skewers with chilli lime sauce

Combine sweet chilli sauce, fish sauce and lime juice in bowl, add chopped thigh fillets; mix well, stand 10 minutes. Thread chicken onto bamboo skewers, cook on heated oiled barbecue until browned and cooked through. Serve topped with sliced green onions.

chutney and mint chicken

Combine grated lemon rind, lemon juice, mango chutney and chopped fresh mint in bowl, add thigh fillets; turn chicken to coat in mixture. Cook chicken on heated oiled barbecue until browned all over and cooked through.

creamy sun-dried tomato pesto chicken

Cook thigh fillets in heated oiled non-stick frying pan until browned; remove from pan. Add sun-dried tomato pesto, chicken stock and cream to pan; cook, stirring, until hot. Return chicken to pan; simmer until chicken is just cooked through. Serve sprinkled with chopped fresh basil.

chicken salsa wraps

Sprinkle thigh fillets with mexican seasoning. Cook on heated oiled grill pan until browned both sides and just cooked through; slice thinly. Heat tortillas according to packet directions. Arrange chicken along centre of each tortilla; top with finely chopped tomato, avocado, red onion and coriander leaves, then drizzle with a little lemon juice; roll tortillas to enclose filling.

chicken with red curry sauce

Spread thigh fillets with a little combined prepared red curry paste and coconut cream. Cook chicken in heated oiled non-stick frying pan until browned on both sides and just cooked through; remove from pan. Add more red curry paste to same pan; cook until fragrant. Add coconut cream, stir until heated. Serve chicken with red curry sauce, topped with chopped fresh basil.

chicken with tomato and herbs

Cook thigh fillets in heated oiled non-stick frying pan until browned and cooked through. Remove from pan; cover to keep warm. Add finely chopped egg tomatoes, olive oil, lemon juice, and chopped fresh dill, parsley and basil; cook over high heat until just heated through. Serve chicken topped with tomato mixture.

chicken, lemon and artichoke skewers

Thread bamboo skewers with chopped thigh fillets, drained canned artichoke hearts, halved, button mushrooms and chopped red capsicum. Cook on heated oiled barbecue until chicken is browned and cooked through, brushing with combined olive oil, lemon juice, crushed garlic and dried oregano during cooking.

barbecue thai chicken

Combine thigh fillets with sweet chilli sauce, crushed garlic, fish sauce, brown sugar and chopped fresh lemon grass. Cook chicken on heated oiled barbecue until browned and cooked through.

tandoori chicken wraps

⅓ cup (100g) tandoori paste
2 tablespoons yogurt
600g chicken tenderloins
6 roti or chapati (280g packet)
cooking-oil spray
2 medium egg tomatoes (150g), sliced thickly
2 lebanese cucumbers (260g), seeded, sliced thinly
50g baby spinach leaves
½ cup (140g) yogurt, extra
½ cup firmly packed fresh mint leaves

Combine tandoori paste and yogurt in medium bowl;
add chicken, toss to coat with tandoori mixture.
Lightly spray roti on both sides with oil spray; cook
on a heated grill plate (or grill or barbecue) on both
sides until browned lightly. Cover to keep warm.
Cook chicken on same heated, oiled grill plate
(or grill or barbecue) until browned and cooked
through; slice thinly.
Divide chicken among the roti, top with tomato,
cucumber, spinach, extra yogurt and mint; roll up
to enclose filling. Cut wraps in half diagonally;
serve warm.

serves 6
per serving 9.8g fat; 1215kJ (290 cal)
on the table in 20 minutes

chicken and chinese broccoli stir-fry

350g fresh singapore noodles
1 tablespoon peanut oil
700g chicken tenderloins, halved
1 large brown onion (200g), sliced thickly
3 cloves garlic, crushed
1kg chinese broccoli, chopped coarsely
⅓ cup (80ml) oyster sauce
1 tablespoon light soy sauce

Rinse noodles in strainer under hot water. Separate noodles with fork; drain.
Heat half of the oil in wok or large frying pan; stir-fry chicken, in batches, until browned all over and cooked through.
Heat remaining oil in wok; stir-fry onion and garlic until onion softens.
Return chicken to wok with broccoli and sauces; stir-fry until broccoli just wilts. Toss chicken mixture with noodles to serve.

serves 4
per serving 10.1g fat; 2266kJ (541 cal)
on the table in 25 minutes
tip Any type of fresh noodle can be used in this recipe.

chicken pitta pockets

8 chicken tenderloins (600g)
2 teaspoons seasoned salt
2 teaspoons olive oil
1 medium brown onion (150g), sliced thinly
¼ cup (75g) mayonnaise
2 teaspoons water
2 teaspoons wholegrain mustard
4 pitta bread pockets
4 green oak leaf lettuce leaves
8 pieces pickled sliced cucumber, drained
2 small egg tomatoes (120g), sliced thinly

Combine chicken and salt in medium bowl; mix well.
Heat oil in large non-stick frying pan; cook onion, stirring, until soft. Remove from pan and keep warm.
Cook chicken in same pan, until browned on both sides and cooked through.
Combine mayonnaise, the water and mustard in small bowl.
Trim each pitta to open. Fill with lettuce, cucumber, chicken, tomato, onion and mayonnaise mixture.

serves 4
per serving 13.9g fat; 2088kJ (336 cal)
on the table in 15 minutes

chicken, pide and haloumi salad

Haloumi is a firm, salty cheese, available from most delicatessens and some supermarkets. Assemble this salad just before serving.

300g prepared mixed vegetable antipasto
500g chicken tenderloins, chopped coarsely
2 tablespoons pine nuts
½ long loaf pide
250g haloumi cheese
200g baby rocket
170g marinated artichoke hearts, drained, quartered
250g cherry tomatoes
¼ cup (60ml) balsamic vinegar

Drain antipasto in strainer over small bowl; reserve ⅓ cup (80ml) of the oil (if there is not enough oil to make ⅓ cup, add olive oil to make up the required amount). Chop antipasto finely.

Heat 1 tablespoon of the reserved oil in wok or large frying pan; stir-fry chicken, in batches, until browned all over and cooked through. Cover to keep warm. Stir-fry pine nuts in wok until lightly browned.

Cut pide into 1cm slices; grill until browned both sides. Cut haloumi crossways into 16 slices. Heat 1 tablespoon of the reserved oil in same wok; cook haloumi, in batches, until browned both sides.

Toss antipasto, chicken, pide and haloumi in large bowl with rocket, artichoke and tomatoes. Drizzle with combined remaining oil and vinegar. Sprinkle with pine nuts.

serves 4
per serving 47.8g fat; 3335kJ (798 cal)
on the table in 25 minutes

warm chicken tabbouleh

1 cup (160g) burghul
600g chicken tenderloins, sliced thinly
2 cloves garlic, crushed
⅔ cup (160ml) lemon juice
¼ cup (60ml) olive oil
250g cherry tomatoes, halved
4 green onions, chopped coarsely
1 cup coarsely chopped fresh flat-leaf parsley
1 cup coarsely chopped fresh mint

Place burghul in small bowl; cover with boiling water. Stand 15 minutes; drain. Using hands, squeeze out as much excess water as possible.
Meanwhile, combine chicken, garlic and 1 tablespoon each of the juice and oil in medium bowl; stand 5 minutes.
Heat 1 tablespoon of the oil in wok or large frying pan; stir-fry chicken mixture, in batches, until chicken is browned all over and cooked through. Cover to keep warm.
Place burghul with tomato and onion in wok; stir-fry until onion softens, remove from heat. Add chicken mixture, parsley, mint, remaining juice and oil; toss gently to combine.

serves 4
per serving 18.1g fat; 1836kJ (439 cal)
on the table in 30 minutes

oven-baked parmesan chicken

Curly endive, also known as frisée, is a loose-headed green vegetable having curly, ragged-edged leaves and a slightly bitter flavour. It is usually used as a salad green, but in Europe it is also eaten as a cooked vegetable.

1 tablespoon plain flour
2 eggs, beaten lightly
2 cups (140g) stale breadcrumbs
⅓ cup (25g) coarsely grated parmesan cheese
2 tablespoons finely chopped fresh flat-leaf parsley
12 chicken tenderloins (900g)
1 cup firmly packed fresh basil leaves
½ cup (125ml) olive oil
¼ cup (60ml) lemon juice
1 clove garlic, quartered
¾ cup (120g) kalamata olives, seeded
200g curly endive
40g baby rocket

Preheat oven to hot.
Combine flour and egg in medium bowl. In another medium bowl combine breadcrumbs, cheese and parsley. Coat chicken, one piece at a time, first in flour mixture then in breadcrumb mixture. Place chicken, in single layer, on oiled oven tray; roast, uncovered, in hot oven about 15 minutes or until chicken is lightly browned and cooked through.
Meanwhile, blend or process basil, oil, juice and garlic until dressing is well combined.
Serve chicken with combined olives, endive and rocket; drizzle with basil dressing.

serves 4
per serving 47.3g fat; 3320kJ (794 cal)
on the table in 30 minutes

even easier tenderloins

chicken satay

Stir-fry sliced tenderloins until browned and cooked through; remove from wok. Add sliced onion and crushed garlic to wok; stir-fry until onion is soft. Return chicken to wok with chicken stock, coconut milk and satay sauce; stir-fry until sauce thickens slightly.

chicken salad with anchovy dressing

Blend or process basil leaves, olive oil, grated parmesan cheese, anchovy fillets and lemon juice until smooth. Combine mixed salad leaves, cherry tomatoes and char-grilled tenderloins; drizzle with anchovy dressing.

chicken with blue-cheese sauce

Combine mayonnaise, crumbled blue cheese, chopped fresh flat-leaf parsley, crushed garlic, lemon juice and enough water to make sauce a pouring consistency. Serve sauce with pan fried or barbecued tenderloins.

salt and pepper tenderloins

Sprinkle tenderloins with lots of cracked black peppercorns, sea salt and lemon pepper seasoning. Stir-fry in heated oiled wok until browned and cooked through. Serve with lemon wedge, if desired.

barbecued chicken with garlic and caper butter

Melt butter in small saucepan; add crushed garlic, capers and chopped fresh oregano. Cook tenderloins on heated oiled barbecue until browned on one side. Turn tenderloins, then spoon over some of the butter mixture; cook until chicken is just cooked through. Serve with remaining butter mixture.

chicken with salsa verde

Combine finely chopped fresh flat-leaf parsley, basil and mint with finely chopped anchovy fillets and capers, crushed garlic, dijon mustard and red wine vinegar; gradually whisk in olive oil. Serve salsa verde spooned over pan-fried or barbecued tenderloins.

chicken with capsicum salsa

Combine finely chopped green capsicum, red onion, red thai chilli, green onion, mint and lemon juice. Serve salsa spooned over pan-fried or barbecued tenderloins.

chicken schnitzels with mayonnaise dressing

Press cornflake crumbs firmly onto tenderloins. Shallow fry schnitzels until browned and cooked through. Combine mayonnaise and sweet fruit chutney. Serve schnitzels with mayonnaise dressing.

glossary

bacon rashers also known as bacon slices; made from cured and smoked pork side.

balsamic vinegar made from white Trebbiano grapes; specially processed then aged in antique wooden casks to give the exquisite pungent flavour.

bean sprouts also known as bean shoots; tender new growths of assorted beans and seeds germinated for consumption as sprouts.

bok choy also known as bak choy, pak choi, chinese white cabbage or chinese chard; has a fresh, mild mustard taste. Use stems and leaves.

burghul also known as bulghur wheat; hulled, steamed wheat kernels. When dried, the grains are crushed into various sizes. Used in Middle-Eastern dishes.

butter use salted or unsalted (sweet) butter; 125g is equal to one stick of butter.

button mushrooms small, cultivated white mushrooms with a mild flavour.

cajun seasoning a blend of assorted herbs and spices that can include paprika, basil, onion, fennel, thyme, cayenne and tarragon.

capers the grey-green buds of a warm climate (usually Mediterranean) shrub, sold either dried and salted or pickled in a vinegar brine. Has a piquant flavour.

capsicum also known as bell pepper or, simply, pepper.

cayenne pepper thin-fleshed, long, extremely hot, dried red chilli, usually purchased ground.

cheese
  blue: mould-treated cheese mottled with blue veining.

brie: has a bloomy white rind and a creamy centre that becomes runnier as it ripens.

gruyère: swiss cheese having small holes and a nutty, slightly salty flavour.

haloumi: firm, cream-coloured sheep-milk cheese matured in brine; somewhat like a minty, salty fetta in flavour.

parmesan: also known as parmigiano, parmesan is a hard, grainy cow-milk cheese.

chicken
  breast fillet: breast halved, skinned and boned.
  tenderloin: thin strip of meat lying just under the breast.
  thigh fillet: has the skin and bone removed.

chickpeas also known as hummus, garbanzos, or channa; an irregularly round, sandy-coloured legume.

chilli available in many types and sizes. Use rubber gloves when seeding and chopping fresh chillies as they can burn your skin. To reduce heat level, remove seeds and membranes.
  red thai: small, medium hot, and bright red in colour.

chinese broccoli also known as gai larn, kanah, gai lum, chinese broccoli and chinese kale; appreciated more for its stems than its coarse leaves.

chinese cabbage also known as peking or napa cabbage, wong bok and petsai. It is elongated in shape with pale green, crinkly leaves.

choy sum a member of the bok choy family; also known as pakaukeo or flowering cabbage. Has long stems, light-green leaves and yellow flowers. Is eaten stems and all.

coconut
  cream: obtained commercially from the first pressing of the coconut flesh, without the addition of water.
  milk: the second pressing of the coconut flesh (less rich) is sold as coconut milk.

coriander also known as pak chee, cilantro or chinese parsley; bright-green leafy herb with a pungent flavour.

cornflake crumbs packaged breadcrumbs made from crushed corn flakes.

cornflour thickening agent, also known as cornstarch.

cos lettuce also known as romaine lettuce.

cumin also known as zeera.

egg noodles also known as yellow noodles; made from wheat flour and eggs, sold fresh and dried. Range in size from very fine strands to wide, thick spaghetti-like pieces.

fish sauce also known as nam pla or nuoc nam; made from pulverised salted fermented fish (most often anchovies). Has pungent smell and strong taste; there are many versions of varying intensity, so use according to your taste.

five-spice powder a fragrant mixture of ground cinnamon, cloves, star anise, sichuan pepper and fennel seeds.

flour, plain an all-purpose flour, made from wheat.

hoisin sauce a thick, sweet and spicy chinese paste made from salted fermented soy beans, onions and garlic.

instant noodles quick-cook noodles also sold as packaged 2-minute noodles, with flavour sachet enclosed.

kaffir lime leaves aromatic leaves of a small citrus tree bearing a wrinkled-skinned green fruit. Used like bay leaves or curry leaves.

kecap manis also known as ketjap manis. A thick soy sauce with added sugar and spices.

lebanese cucumber short, slender and thin-skinned; also known as the european or burpless cucumber.

lemon grass a tall, clumping, lemon-smelling and -tasting, sharp-edged grass; the white lower part of the stem is used, finely chopped, in cooking.

lemon pepper seasoning a blend of crushed black pepper, lemon, herbs and spices.

lentils (red, brown, yellow) dried pulses often identified by and named after their colour.

madras curry paste packaged versions consist of coriander, cumin, pepper, turmeric, chilli, garlic, ginger, vinegar and oil.

mexican seasoning a blend of chilli powder, paprika, cumin, oregano, pepper and garlic.

mustard

dijon: pale brown, distinctively flavoured, fairly mild tasting french mustard.

wholegrain: also known as seeded mustard. French-style coarse-grain mustard made from crushed mustard seeds and dijon-style french mustard.

oak leaf lettuce also known as Feville de Chene. Available in both red and green leaf.

oil

olive: made from ripened olives. Extra virgin and virgin are the best. Extra light or light refers to taste not fat levels.

peanut: pressed from ground peanuts; commonly used in Asian cooking because of its high smoke point (handles high heat without burning).

vegetable: any of a number of oils sourced from plants rather than animal fats.

onion

green: also known as scallion or, incorrectly, shallot.

red: also known as spanish, red spanish or bermuda onion; a sweet-flavoured, large, purple-red onion.

oyster sauce made from oysters and their brine, cooked with salt and soy sauce, and thickened with starches.

paprika ground, dried red capsicum (bell pepper); available sweet or hot.

parsley, flat-leaf also known as continental or italian parsley.

pide comes in long (about 45cm) flat loaves as well as individual rounds; made from wheat flour and sprinkled with sesame or black onion seeds.

pine nuts also known as pignoli.

pitta bread also known as lebanese bread. Wheat-flour pocket bread sold in large, flat pieces that separate into two thin rounds, or as small thick pieces called pocket pitta.

prosciutto cured, air-dried (unsmoked), pressed ham.

red curry paste a combination of dried red chillies, onions, garlic, oil, lemon rind, shrimp paste, ground cumin, paprika, ground turmeric and ground black pepper.

rice noodles, fresh can be purchased in various widths or large sheets. They do not need pre-cooking.

rocket also known as arugula, rugula and rucola; a green, peppery-tasting leaf.

sambal oelek (also ulek or olek); a salty paste made from ground chillies and vinegar.

satay sauce spicy peanut sauce served with grilled meat skewers.

seasoned salt combine ½ teaspoon five-spice powder with 2 tablespoons coarse kitchen salt in heavy-based pan. Stir over low heat for 2 minutes.

soy sauce also known as sieu, is made from fermented soy beans. We used a mild Japanese variety.

spinach also known as english spinach and, incorrectly, silverbeet.

stock concentrated liquid, cubes or powder can be used. As a guide, 1 teaspoon of stock powder or 1 small crumbled stock cube or 1 portion stock concentrate mixed with 1 cup (250ml) water will give a fairly strong stock.

sun-dried tomato pesto made from sun-dried tomatoes, oil, vinegar and herbs.

telegraph cucumber long and green with ridges running down its entire length; also known as continental cucumber.

teriyaki sauce usually made from soy sauce, mirin, sugar, ginger and other spices.

tikka masala paste consisting of chilli, coriander, cumin, lentil flour, garlic, ginger, oil, turmeric, fennel, pepper, cloves, cinnamon and cardamom.

turmeric, ground also known as kamin; imparts a golden colour when added to dishes.

index

conversion chart

MEASURES

One Australian metric measuring cup holds approximately 250ml, one Australian metric tablespoon holds 20ml, one Australian metric teaspoon holds 5ml.

The difference between one country's measuring cups and another's is within a two- or three-teaspoon variance, and will not affect your cooking results. North America, New Zealand and the United Kingdom use a 15ml tablespoon.

All cup and spoon measurements are level. The most accurate way of measuring dry ingredients is to weigh them. When measuring liquids, use a clear glass or plastic jug with the metric markings.

We use large eggs with an average weight of 60g.

DRY MEASURES

METRIC	IMPERIAL
15g	½oz
30g	1oz
60g	2oz
90g	3oz
125g	4oz (¼lb)
155g	5oz
185g	6oz
220g	7oz
250g	8oz (½lb)
280g	9oz
315g	10oz
345g	11oz
375g	12oz (¾lb)
410g	13oz
440g	14oz
470g	15oz
500g	16oz (1lb)
750g	24oz (1½lb)
1kg	32oz (2lb)

LIQUID MEASURES

METRIC	IMPERIAL
30ml	1 fluid oz
60ml	2 fluid oz
100ml	3 fluid oz
125ml	4 fluid oz
150ml	5 fluid oz (¼ pint/1 gill)
190ml	6 fluid oz
250ml	8 fluid oz
300ml	10 fluid oz (½ pint)
500ml	16 fluid oz
600ml	20 fluid oz (1 pint)
1000ml (1 litre)	1¾ pints

LENGTH MEASURES

METRIC	IMPERIAL
3mm	⅛in
6mm	¼in
1cm	½in
2cm	¾in
2.5cm	1in
5cm	2in
6cm	2½in
8cm	3in
10cm	4in
13cm	5in
15cm	6in
18cm	7in
20cm	8in
23cm	9in
25cm	10in
28cm	11in
30cm	12in (1ft)

OVEN TEMPERATURES

These oven temperatures are only a guide for conventional ovens. For fan-forced ovens, check the manufacturer's manual.

	°C (CELSIUS)	°F (FAHRENHEIT)	GAS MARK
Very slow	120	250	½
Slow	150	275 – 300	1 – 2
Moderately slow	160	325	3
Moderate	180	350 – 375	4 – 5
Moderately hot	200	400	6
Hot	220	425 – 450	7 – 8
Very hot	240	475	9

Are you missing some of the world's favourite cookbooks

The Australian Women's Weekly cookbooks are available from bookshops, cookshops, supermarkets and other stores all over the world. You can also buy direct from the publisher, using the order form below.

MINI SERIES £3.50 190x138MM 64 PAGES

TITLE	QTY	TITLE	QTY	TITLE	QTY
4 Fast Ingredients		Drinks		Party Food	
15-minute Feasts		Fast Fish		Pasta	
30-minute Meals		Fast Food for Friends		Pickles and Chutneys	
50 Fast Chicken Fillets		Fast Soup		Potatoes	
After-work Stir-fries		Finger Food		Risotto	
Barbecue		Gluten-free Cooking		Roast	
Barbecue Chicken		Healthy Everyday Food 4 Kids		Salads	
Barbecued Seafood		Ice-creams & Sorbets		Simple Slices	
Biscuits, Brownies & Biscotti		Indian Cooking		Simply Seafood	
Bites		Indonesian Favourites		Skinny Food	
Bowl Food		Italian		Stir-fries	
Burgers, Rösti & Fritters		Italian Favourites		Summer Salads	
Cafe Cakes		Jams & Jellies		Tapas, Antipasto & Mezze	
Cafe Food		Kids Party Food		Thai Cooking	
Casseroles		Last-minute Meals		Thai Favourites	
Char-grills & Barbecues		Lebanese Cooking		The Packed Lunch	
Cheesecakes, Pavlova & Trifles		Low Fat Fast		Vegetarian	
Chinese Favourites		Malaysian Favourites		Vegetarian Stir-fries	
Chocolate Cakes		Mince Favourites		Vegie Main Meals	
Christmas Cakes & Puddings		Mince		Wok	
Cocktails		Muffins		Young Chef	
Crumbles & Bakes		Noodles		TOTAL COST	£
Curries		Outdoor Eating			

Photocopy and complete coupon below

Name _____

Address _____

_____ Postcode _____

Country _____ Phone (business hours) _____

Email*(optional) _____

* By including your email address, you consent to receipt of any email regarding this magazine, and other emails which inform you of ACP's other publications, products, services and events, and to promote third party goods and services you may be interested in.

I enclose my cheque/money order for £ _____ or please charge £ _____

to my: ☐ Access ☐ Mastercard ☐ Visa ☐ Diners Club
PLEASE NOTE: WE DO NOT ACCEPT SWITCH OR ELECTRON CARDS

Card number | | | | | | | | | | | | | | | | |

3 digit security code *(found on reverse of card)* _____

Cardholder's signature _____ Expiry date ____ /____

To order: Mail or fax – photocopy or complete the order form above, and send your credit card details or cheque payable to: Australian Consolidated Press (UK), Moulton Park Business Centre, Red House Road, Moulton Park, Northampton NN3 6AQ, phone (+44) (0) 1 604 497531, fax (+44) (0) 1 604 497533, e-mail books@acpmedia.co.uk. Or order online at www.acpuk.com
Non-UK residents: We accept the credit cards listed on the coupon, or cheques, drafts or International Money Orders payable in sterling and drawn on a UK bank. Credit card charges are at the exchange rate current at the time of payment.
All pricing current at time of going to press and subject to change/availability.
Postage and packing UK: Add £1.00 per order plus 25p per book.
Postage and packing overseas: Add £2.00 per order plus 50p per book. Offer ends 31.12.2007